Published by Saunders Book Company
27 Stewart Road
Collingwood ON Canada L9Y 4M7

Design and production by The Design Lab
Art direction by Rita Marshall
Printed in the United States of America

Photographs by 123RF (Nattthawat Wongrat),
Corbis (John Conrad, Randy Wells), Dreamstime
(Napy8gen), Getty Images (Theo Allofs, Altrendo
Nature, Chris Baker, P. Kumar, Thorsten Milse,
Schafer & Hill, Gary Vestal), iStockphoto (Vinod
Bartakk, Derek Dammann, Eric Isselee, Keith
Livingston)

Library of Congress Cataloging-in-Publication Data
Bodden, Valerie.
Tigers / by Valerie Bodden.
p. cm. — (Amazing animals)
Includes bibliographical references.
ISBN 978-1-897563-69-4
1. Tigers—Juvenile literature. I. Title.

QL737.C23B635 2009
599.756—dc22   2007051591

CG 12/15/10 PO002379
9 8 7 6 5 4 3

AMAZING ANIMALS

TIGERS

BY VALERIE BODDEN

SAUNDERS
BOOK COMPANY

Tigers are big cats. They live in the wild. There used to be eight kinds of tigers. But some of them died out. Today, there are only five kinds of tigers left.

Tigers are the only big cats that have striped fur

Most tigers are orange with black stripes. But some tigers are white with black stripes. All tigers have white fur on their bellies, throats, and legs. Tigers have big teeth. They have long, sharp claws.

Tigers have strong teeth and big paws with claws

Tigers are the biggest cats in the world. If a tiger stood on its back feet, it would be much taller than a grown-up man! Male tigers can weigh more than 500 pounds (227 kg). Female tigers are smaller.

Tigers are big animals, but they can jump high

Tigers that live in snowy places have thick fur

Tigers live on the continent of Asia. Some tigers live in forests. It is cold in some of the forests. There can be a lot of snow there. Other tigers live in swamps. It is warm in the swamps.

continent one of Earth's seven big pieces of land

swamps areas of land that are wet and have lots of trees

All tigers eat meat. They like to eat deer and pigs. Some tigers eat monkeys, too. A few tigers have eaten people.

Tigers move quietly when they try to catch food

Tiger cubs hide while their mother hunts for food

Female tigers have two to four cubs at a time. At first, the cubs drink their mother's milk. Then she teaches them to hunt. The cubs leave their mother by the time they are three years old. Wild tigers can live for 10 to 15 years.

cubs baby tigers

Tigers sometimes sneak through grass to hunt

Grown tigers live alone. They sleep most of the day. At night, they get up. If they are hungry, they hunt for **prey**.

prey animals that are eaten by other animals

Tigers make different sounds. They can make a quiet "chuff" sound through their noses. They can growl and snarl, too. And they can roar very loud.

Tigers may roar to tell
other tigers to stay away

Today, tigers are kept in lots of zoos. People all over the world like to watch tigers. It is exciting to see these big cats eat, sleep, and play!

Many people go to zoos to see tigers and other cats

A *Tiger Story*

Why do tigers have stripes? People in Asia used to tell a story about this. They said that the tiger asked a man for wisdom. The man said he had to go get the wisdom. He did not want the tiger to eat his goats. So he used ropes to tie the tiger to a tree while he was gone. The tiger tried to get out of the ropes. Pulling on the ropes made them dig into his fur and leave stripes on it!

Read More

Suen, Anastasia. *A Tiger Grows Up*. Minneapolis:
Picture Window Books, 2006.

Thomson, Sarah. *Amazing Tigers*. New York:
HarperCollins, 2004.

Web Sites

Enchanted Learning: Tiger
http://www.enchantedlearning.com/subjects/mammals/tiger/Tigertocolor.shtml
This site has tiger facts and a picture to color.

National Zoo: Great Cats
http://nationalzoo.si.edu/Animals/GreatCats/catskids.cfm?nzps=see
This site has big cat activities and games.

Index